MY FIRST
HALLOWEEN
BOOK

by Colleen L. Reece
illustrated by Pam Peltier

created by The Child's World

℗ CHILDRENS PRESS ™

CHICAGO

DEDICATION

for Jennifer

Susan

Rebecca

with love from Colleen

Library of Congress Cataloging in Publication Data

Reece, Colleen L.
   My first Halloween book.

   Summary: focuses on various Halloween themes, including
trick-or-treat, witches, haunted houses, and monsters.
   1. Children's poetry, American. 2. Halloween—
Juvenile poetry. [1. Halloween-Poetry. 2. American
poetry] I. Peltier, Pam, ill. II. Child's World (Firm)
PS3568.E3646M95 1984   811'.54   84-9431
ISBN 0-516-02902-9

MY FIRST

HALLOWEEN
BOOK

Halloween

Orange and black streamers
from ceiling to floor.
Big jack-o-lanterns
beside the front door.
So many cornstalks
there's no room for more.
　　It's plain to be seen,
　　it's HALLOWEEN.

Spooks

Ghosts and goblins,
witches and spooks,
found inside
my picture books.
Scary and ugly,
they moan and scream,
and come out to play
on Halloween.

Dressing Up

Dressing up for Halloween
is so much fun!
I can be a cowboy
   or a clown.
I can be a princess
   or a pirate.
I can even be E.T.
When I'm dressed up,
you won't know me.

Trick-or-Treat

I like to knock on doors
and say, "Trick-or-treat!"
When the people ask,
   "Who are you?"
sometimes I say, "BOO!"

Parties

I wish Halloween
    were every day
    and not just one.
We get to drink warm cider
    and eat doughnuts
        and bob for apples.
Everyone gets wet, but that's okay.
Halloween parties are fun.

Witches

Wicked Old Witch
   has a long black cape,
     a pointy hat,
     and stringy hair.
She rides through the air
   on a magic broom.
In her one-room house
        is a
steaming kettle of witches brew.
She found her pets
   when the Night Wind blew—
     bats
       and toads
         and a giant mouse.

Black Cats

My cat Mandrake is a
   Halloween cat.
He has big green eyes,
and shiny black fur that
   makes sparks
   in the dark. . .
   if I pet him the wrong way.
But it's funny.
If I put a sheet
   over my head,
Mandrake meows
   and crawls under the bed!

Scarecrows

When the only light
is the yellow moon . . .
and black cats and bats and rats
and witches on brooms go by—
    does the scarecrow
    under the Halloween sky
      ever get scared?
Or wish that someone other than
a grinning orange pumpkin
would keep him company?

    He should.
    I would!

Jack-O'-Lanterns

Pumpkins are jack-o'-lanterns
that haven't been made yet.
They need Dad to
    take out the seeds,
    and give them eyes,
        a nose,
        a mouth,
        even teeth
so they can smile.

Haunted Houses

The empty house across the street
    looks lonely.
It's only on Halloween that
    people say it's haunted.
        Chains rattle.
        Boards creak.
        There are funny squeaks.
My brother says he's seen
    a bony finger waving
    out of a broken window—
        and heard a voice calling,
            "Ooo — Ooo — Ooo."
        It scared him, too.

Squirrels

The squirrels who live
in our big oak tree,
   aren't like me.
I get to trick-or-treat.
   But. . .
they have to store up nuts
   and acorns.
If I put some in the yard,
the squirrels won't have to
         work so hard.

Owls

High in the bare branches
of a crooked tree,
a yellow-eyed owl
  watches me.
    "Whoo-whoo?" he cries.
The Night Wind catches and sighs,
    "Whoo-whoo."
I run into the house
and lock the door,
so they can't ask me any more,
    "Whoo-whoo?"

Monsters

Mother says monsters aren't real,
   just pretend.
I know she's right.
   But when we all dress up
   and, as scary creatures,
   run into the night, crying,
     "Trick-or-treat,"
   sometimes I forget.
At the end of Halloween,
   we take off our masks.
     I'm glad.
The monsters really are my friends.

History

I asked Mom,
　　"Who made Halloween?"
She smiled and said,
　　"Terry, long ago
　　people thought fairies
　　　　and elves
　　　　　and witches
　　　　were real.
　　So they built big bonfires
　　to scare them away.
　　They told ghost stories
　　just as we do."
I'm glad.
I like Halloween—
　　and ghost stories, too.